Noelle Sorensen

A Knife

to a

Gunfight

i

came

with love

as my weapon

hands trembling but

honest. you brought

a war i never asked

for. but still — i stood

sharp. silver-tongued.

tip to handle.

quiet fury

in a world

that only

honors

the loud.

— a knife to

a gunfight

Table of Contents

The Glance

before you walked in

i was
quietly
healing

drinking
my coffee
with both hands

not hoping
for anything

but peace

and then
the door opened

and every part of me
that had finally
gone still

started
shaking
again

the air shifted

i didn't
see you

but i felt
you

like the room
took
a sharp inhale
and held it

my skin
tightened
like a truth
i hadn't told yet

everything
was the same
except

me

my eyes found you too fast

i wasn't
looking

but there you were
like a secret
that had been waiting
to be seen

too soon
too sudden
too much

my gaze
tripped over you
and forgot
how to walk away

something sharp beneath your smile

you smiled
but it didn't
reach
your eyes

there was something
hidden there
like a blade
waiting
to cut the silence

i pretended
i didn't notice
but my body
knew better
it shivered
and leaned back

just in case

we weren't introduced / but i knew you

there was no name
no handshake
no shared history

but my heart
had heard your footsteps
before you arrived

you carried something
familiar
like a memory
i hadn't lived yet

and in that moment
i knew
exactly
who you were
even before you knew me

i looked away second

just long enough
to convince myself
i wasn't
feeling
what i was feeling

but in that second

i knew
i had already
lost
the battle

because you didn't need
to look back
for me
to follow

a stillness i didn't trust

there was quiet
and for a moment
i thought
maybe it was peace

but something
in the air
shifted

too quickly
too heavy

i realized
i was waiting
for the storm
that always
comes after calm

you moved like a question

everything about you was unsure but full of curiosity i wondered if you were asking if i could love you or if i could let you go but i never got the answer because i couldn't

ﾂ

the moment was small / but it stayed

a glance

a touch

a word
spoken softly

it wasn't enough
to make a difference

yet it stayed
like an echo
in my chest

every time
i tried to forget
it came back
louder than before

your laugh had an edge

it sounded like joy
          but it cut
like something sharp

i didn't know
whether to smile
          or flinch
because in that sound
was both warmth
          and warning

you wore it
          like armor
and i couldn't decide
if i wanted to hold you
                                        or run

you stared like you meant it

your gaze wasn't casual
like it usually is

it was steady
searching
like you had something to find
in the depths of me

and for a second
i thought
maybe i had
something to hide

but i held it—
the stare
the silence
the weight

and you didn't look away

until i did

the room leaned toward you

it wasn't just your voice
or the way you stood
    with the world at your feet

the air itself moved closer
like it wanted to hear
    every word you said

i tried to listen
but the room kept turning toward you
            and i couldn't turn it back

danger dressed like curiosity

you asked questions
like you didn't know
the answers were risks

you smiled
like you weren't
testing my boundaries
with every word

i should've known better
but your eyes
looked so innocent
i didn't see the storm coming

until it was already here

the first time i forgot myself

i didn't notice
until i couldn't hear
my own voice
in the noise of you

you asked questions
and i answered
but the answers
weren't mine
they were yours
wrapped in my skin

it felt like freedom
but it was only forgetting
and in that moment
i became someone
else's reflection

i didn't believe in signs / until then

but there you were
like the universe
finally speaking my language

the way you smiled
the way you moved
felt like the answer
i had been searching for
in all the wrong places

and for the first time
i didn't question
i just followed
where you led

you blinked / i broke

a moment
so small
it went unnoticed
by everyone
but me

you blinked
and in that instant
i shattered
like glass
too fragile to hold
the weight of your absence

my skin noticed first

before my heart
or my mind
could catch up

it tingled
when you were near
and pulled away
when you were gone

it remembered
the heat of your touch
before I ever could

my body
always knew
what I refused
to admit

your voice across the room

it wasn't loud
but it found me
like it always does

in the crowd
your words
were soft
but every syllable
carried weight

i didn't need to see you
to feel you
because your voice
wrapped around me
and made the air
hold its breath

i stopped making sense

the words

tangled in my throat

like knots i couldn't
untie

i tried to speak
but the silence

was LOUDER
than my thoughts

i didn't know
who i was anymore

or why
i was still
waiting for you
to understand

you walked past / i followed

i didn't ask
if i should

but my feet
moved

before my mind
could decide

you didn't look back
but my heart knew

the direction

without question

i followed
like a promise

i wasn't ready to keep

i pretended not to care

but every time
you looked away
i felt
the emptiness
fill me up
like a storm
i couldn't outrun

i wore indifference
like armor
but my heart
knew the truth
it bled
even when my lips
said nothing

you saw through it

the mask i wore
the silence i carried
you saw past
the walls i built
and into
the trembling me

you didn't ask
for my truths
but you knew them
anyway
and in your gaze
i found the courage
to speak them out loud

you smiled like you knew something

like there was a secret
tucked behind your teeth
a truth
i wasn't ready
to hear

your smile held
a thousand unspoken words
and for a moment
i wondered
if you were the answer
i had been searching for
in all the wrong places

i didn't know what i wanted / until you stood there

like there was a secret
tucked behind your teeth
a truth
i wasn't ready
to hear

your smile held
a thousand unspoken words
and for a moment
i wondered
if you were the answer
i had been searching for

i didn't know what i wanted / until you stood there

before you,
everything felt
like a question
without an answer

but the moment
you stood in front of me,
i realized
i was already searching
for you
in the spaces
i didn't know

i was empty

the lights flickered / or maybe i did

the moment
your eyes found mine,
everything felt
unsteady
like the world
was unsure
if it should stay still
or move

i didn't know
if it was the lights
or if it was me
shaking
for the first time
in years

not love / not yet / but something

it wasn't the kind of feeling
that could be named
or held down
by any word

but it was there
growing between us
like a seed
waiting for the right moment
to bloom

not love—

not yet—

but something

deep enough to make
me wonder
if this was the beginning
of all the things
we hadn't said

something old and dangerous

it wasn't the spark
that caught me

but the weight
of something familiar
in your eyes

like we had met
in another lifetime
and unfinished business
had followed us here

you didn't ask me
to walk with you

but the pull
was impossible
to ignore

the first mistake i wanted to make twice

it wasn't just a slip
or a choice
it was the way
you made me feel
like breaking the rules
wasn't a risk
but a promise

i knew better
but i let myself
fall anyway
because sometimes
the first mistake
feels like the only
truth

you didn't touch me / but it felt like you did

your presence
was enough
to make the air heavy
and my skin tingle
like you were already there
without ever reaching for me

i couldn't tell
if it was your gaze
or the space
you left between us
but something about it
felt like a touch
i couldn't escape

that look started the war

your eyes
didn't ask for permission
they took
everything
they wanted
and left me
fighting with myself
to decide
if i would
surrender

or resist

The Pull

i kept finding reasons to stay

every time
i tried to leave
you gave me
a half-smile
a soft word
a memory
i wasn't ready
to let go of

so i stayed
not because it was right
but because it was
familiar

your name sat heavy in my mouth

i tried to speak it
like it didn't mean anything
but it came out
like a confession

soft
slow
trembling with
everything i couldn't say

your name
was never just a name
it was a memory
a wound
a wish
i hadn't made yet

i swore i wouldn't text you

i told myself
i had dignity
i had strength
i had moved on

but at 2:13 a.m.
loneliness wore me down
and your name
looked too easy
on the screen

i didn't say much

just

hey

but we both knew
what that meant

some promises
aren't made
to be kept

but i did

i said i wouldn't
reach out
think of you
miss you

i told myself
i was stronger
than the ache

but strength
isn't always silence
and healing
isn't always clean

so i did
text you
miss you
want you
and maybe
that was part
of letting go

you said the right thing / at the wrong time

the words
i waited months to hear
finally left your mouth
just as
i stopped listening

you reached for me
when i had
already learned
how to stand
without your hand

and isn't that
how it always is—
love shows up
once the door
has already

closed

it didn't feel like a choice

loving you
wasn't something
i decided

i tried to walk away slower

as if dragging my feet
would undo the goodbye

as if taking smaller steps
would make you
change your mind

i left like i wanted
you to stop me
but you stood still
like letting go
was easy

so i kept walking
pretending
every step
didn't break
a little more of me

you never asked / but i gave

you didn't reach for me

but i opened anyway

like a door
waiting to be noticed

i handed you
pieces of myself
wrapped in quiet hope
and soft excuses

you never asked

but i gave

as if love could be built

one-sided

as if maybe
you'd love me in return

just out of gratitude

every no turned into maybe

i built boundaries
with trembling hands
whispered no
like a prayer
i didn't believe in

but you smiled
and suddenly
no felt too heavy
to carry

so i softened
my edges
bent my spine
rearranged my truth
to make room
for your comfort

until maybe
became yes
and i couldn't remember
where i ended

the quiet between our messages

you didn't say much
but silence
has a sound
when you care enough
to listen

i waited hours
for your typing bubble
like it might spell
something different
this time

but it never did

you spoke in pauses

and i translated them
into hope
when i should have
read them

as goodbye

i answered before i thought

before i could catch
the words
i had already let them slip
like secrets
i wasn't ready to share

my heart
spoke faster than my mind
and my mouth
didn't know how
to stop it

i said yes
when i should have said no
because sometimes
the feeling
is louder than the truth

you knew how to reel me in

you spoke in riddles
and i was desperate
for the answers

your words
tangled my thoughts
until i couldn't remember
where i ended
and you began

i swam deeper
into your pull
believing i could outrun
the undertow.

but all along
you were the one
holding the line

your voice was a rope

it tangled around me
pulling me closer
until i couldn't breathe
without it

i told myself
i was strong enough
to break free
but each word
wrapped tighter
like it knew
exactly how to hold me

and when i tried to escape
it was your voice
that pulled me back
like it was always
meant to be
my anchor

i ignored the warnings

they whispered at first
small voices
hidden in the back of my mind

but you smiled
and suddenly
their truth felt too heavy
for me to carry

so i chose to listen
to the noise you made

and ignored
the silence that knew better

until the storm came
and i had nowhere to hide

because it felt good

i stayed too long
in the heat of something
that burned
but warmed me
at the same time

i knew it wasn't right
but there was a comfort
in the chaos
and a softness
in the way you broke me

so i kept coming back
because it felt good
even when
it shouldn't have

because it felt like fire

i danced too close
to the flames
knowing they would burn
but there was something
in the heat
that made me feel alive

each touch
each word
felt like an ember
sparked by something
i couldn't resist

and though i knew
it would scar me
i couldn't stop
because it felt like fire
and fire was
the only thing
that ever made me feel
this awake

i stopped talking about you / to keep you mine

i learned silence
was the only way
to protect
what was still mine
even if you never asked
to be kept

i hid our stories
in the spaces
between my breath
because sharing them
would've made them real
and i wasn't ready
to let go of the fantasy

that maybe
you were always meant
to be
only mine

my hands kept reaching

even when
i knew better
even when
i had been burned
before

my hands kept reaching
for something
that felt like home
even if it was only
an illusion

i wanted
to believe
that this time
it would be different
that the warmth
would stay
and not turn
to ash again

you made danger sound like love

with every word
you spun a story
where chaos felt like comfort
and risk felt like home

you kissed the edge
of everything
i was afraid of
and made me believe
it was the safest place
i could ever be

you made danger
feel like warmth
like something
i couldn't resist
even if it broke me
in the end

i was addicted to the chase

it wasn't you
it was the thrill
of reaching for something
that always felt
just out of my grasp

i learned to love
the hunt
more than the capture
because every step
felt like victory
even if i never
caught you

i convinced myself
the chase was enough

but in the end
it left me
empty

and still chasing
something i never wanted

to catch

you pulled / i leaned

like gravity
made us inevitable
you reached
and i followed
without question

i swore it wasn't love / but it looked like it

i told myself
it was just a spark
just a passing moment
nothing to hold on to

but every touch
felt like more
every glance
felt like a promise

i swore it wasn't love
but it looked like it
in the way you held me
in the way my heart
waited for you

the way you said come over

wasn't an invitation
it was a command
wrapped in sweetness
and my name
spoken softly
like a secret only I
was meant to know

it wasn't the words
but the way they landed
on my skin
like a question
i couldn't refuse
and I was already
moving toward you
before I knew
if I even wanted to

i kept saying yes

even when
i knew the answer
should have been no

i kept saying yes
because your eyes
made me feel
like i was wanted
like i mattered
in a world
that often forgot me

i kept saying yes
until it felt like
a habit
until saying no
became a foreign word
i didn't know how to speak

my heart skipped / but not from feare

it wasn't the thrill
of danger
or the weight of uncertainty
that made my pulse race

it was the way
you looked at me
like i was something
you wanted to keep
like i was enough
and nothing more was needed

my heart skipped
because i felt seen
not afraid
just
something in me
finally felt
home

you made it easy to forget myself

you whispered my name
like it was the only thing
that mattered
and in your eyes
i saw a version of me
that felt
more alive
than the one i knew

i let go
of everything i thought
i needed to be
just to be with you
and in your presence
i became
someone i didn't recognize

every touch was a promise

each time your fingers brushed mine
it was a vow
spoken without words
a whisper in the space
between us

you didn't have to say
i'll stay
i heard it in the way
your hands lingered
on my skin
like they were
claiming me

and for a moment
i believed you
because every touch
felt like something
i could trust

every promise was a trap

you said you'd never leave
and i believed
you'd always stay
but promises
are just words
we say to hold someone close

each one you made
was a thread
wrapped around me
tighter and tighter
until i couldn't breathe
without your love

but love
wasn't freedom
it was a cage
and i never saw it
until i was trapped

you never had to ask twice

when you wanted something
i gave it to you
without hesitation
because your eyes
were enough to make me
forget myself
forget my own needs

you never had to ask twice
and i didn't question
why

because loving you
felt like breathing
even when it took all
of my air

i was already falling

before you even knew
how to catch me
i was already falling
into something i couldn't name
but felt
in every breath i took
in every glance
you gave me

you didn’t pull me in
i was already lost
in the gravity
of your presence
and by the time
you noticed
i was already
too far gone

The Hit

thoughts
swirl
endlessly...
swirl
thoughts
endlessly...
swirl
thoughts
endlessly...
swirl
thoughts
endlessly...
swirl
thoughts
swirl
endlessly...
swirl
thoughts
endlessly...
swirl
thoughts
endlessly...
swirl
thoughts
endlessly...
swirl
thoughts
swirl
endlessly...
swirl
thoughts
endlessly...

i fell before i landed

i thought i had time
to catch my breath
but you pulled me
into the fall
before i could even
brace myself

the ground was still
miles away
and yet
i was already
crashing
into everything
i thought i could avoid

and in that moment
i realized
i had never really been
in control
of my own descent

you said you'd catch me

when the fall felt too fast
when the ground felt too far
you promised
you would be there
to soften the blow

but promises
are only as strong
as the hands
that hold them

and when i hit the earth
i realized
you were never
close enough

to keep me from
shattering

i didn't ask where

when you offered me your hand
i didn't ask where we were going
i just followed
because the road felt safe
beneath your feet

i didn't need directions
or promises
i only needed
the warmth of your touch
to guide me
through the dark

but as we kept walking
i realized
sometimes the destination
wasn't as important
as the steps we took
to get there

the room spun when you touched me

like your fingers
were the only thing
keeping the world
from falling apart

each time your skin
brushed mine
the air shifted
and everything i thought i knew
fell into chaos

i lost my balance
but somehow
i didn't want to find it
because for the first time
the world felt alive
in ways i couldn't explain
but didn't need to

your hands were a fever

they burned
with a heat
that left me trembling
even after you pulled away

each touch
was a fire
i didn't know how to put out
and every second
i spent in your grip
felt like both
too much
and never enough

i tried to resist
but your touch
was an illness
i didn't want to heal from

we were fire / we were flood

we burned each other
until nothing was left
but ash in our lungs

but in the same breath
we drowned each other
in a storm we couldn't escape
pulling each other under
with every kiss

we were both destruction
and salvation
two forces colliding
too close to ever be
anything but
dangerous

there was no safe word

no line to draw
no word to say
when the world you built
became too much to bear

you pushed
and pulled
and every time i gasped
it felt like love
but love didn't hurt
the way you did

i couldn't stop myself
from falling deeper
because the danger felt like desire
and desire felt like drowning
but i didn't have a way out
because there was no safe word
and i wasn't ready to leave yet

you loved me like a warning

like every word
was a siren
screaming
stay away
and every kiss
felt like
a countdown
to something i couldn't undo

you loved me
with a fear in your eyes
like you knew
i was something
too dangerous
to hold
but you held me anyway
and let the storm rage
inside us both

i answered like a match

one spark
and everything ignited
i didn't even think
before i let myself burn
for you

you struck me
with a look
and i lit up
faster than i could control
because your fire
felt like everything
i had been searching for
even if it would destroy me
in the end

the bed became a battlefield

we fought in whispers
in touches that turned
into wounds
in love
that felt like war

each word
cut deeper than the last
and every kiss
was both surrender
and attack

we weren't fighting each other
we were fighting
the truth
we didn't want to see
that we were never
meant to win

we broke things just to feel them

the way glass shatters
is a kind of release
so we broke promises
and hearts
just to see the pieces fall
and hear the sound
of something
finally breaking open

we let our hands
destroy what we once held close
because sometimes
the only way to know
we were alive
was to feel
s
o
m
e
t
h
i
n
g
fall
apart

your name hit like lightning

it wasn't the sound
but the sudden shock
that took me by surprise
like a storm
i didn't see coming

your name
spoken once
was enough
to light up the sky
and leave me
burning in its wake

i couldn't look away
even as the thunder
rattled my bones
because i knew
this was a force
too powerful to resist

we kissed like we meant to hurt

our lips crashed together
not for love
but for something darker
something that felt like
retribution
and release

we didn't care
about tenderness
or the breaking
of what was once whole
we kissed
because it was the only way
we knew how to
feel
everything we were
too afraid to admit

your silence burned louder than your voice

when you stopped speaking
the room filled with everything
you didn't say
it was louder than any word
could have been
sharp
like a knife hidden in the quiet

your silence told me more
than your promises ever did
it whispered truths
i wasn't ready to hear
and when you looked away
it felt like the world
was unraveling
just beneath my feet

you fed the parts of me that starved

you didn't give me what i wanted

you gave me what i needed

the things i had buried

the hunger i had ignored

you fed the pieces of me

i had learned to live without

in your touch
i found the warmth
i had been searching for

and in your words
i tasted the love
i never thought i deserved

you didn't just fill the empty spaces

you made me whole again

then called me greedy

after you fed me
the love i never knew how to ask for
after you made me whole
in ways i didn't know i needed
you called me greedy
for wanting more
for wanting to keep
the parts of you
that fit me so perfectly

but i didn't ask for this hunger
it was yours
you lit the fire
and then blamed me
for trying to keep it burning

i blurred myself to stay

i tried to shrink
into your world
to be small enough
to fit your silence
to blend into the space
you didn't want to fill

i blurred the edges of who i was
until i couldn't tell
where i ended
and you began
because the longer i stayed
the less i knew
if i was staying for you
or staying because
i had forgotten
how to leave

you pulled me in with apologies

you whispered them
like they were promises
like they could heal
what you had broken
but they were just words
spilled out too easily
without the weight
of change behind them

i let myself believe
they were enough
to make me whole again
but apologies
can only hold you
for so long
before you realize
the cracks
were never fixed

just covered up

then pushed me out with indifference

you didn't need to raise your voice
you didn't need to say a thing
your silence was enough
to make me feel
like i never mattered
in the first place

you didn't care
if i stayed or left
and that was the worst part
because the love you gave
was never really love
it was just something
to fill the empty spaces
until you grew tired of it

i started lying to my friends

telling them i was fine
when i wasn't
telling them i had moved on
when i still couldn't let go

you started lying to me

because it was easier
than facing what we were
but lies only stretch so far
before they snap
and leave everything
exposed

the love was real / the damage more so

we loved like it was all we had
with everything we could give
but somewhere between the passion
and the promises
we lost ourselves

the love was raw
and real
but it came with scars
we didn't know how to heal

and when the dust settled
the damage was clearer
than the love we swore
would save us

we gave everything
and in the end
we were left
holding pieces
of what we could never fix

you never hit me / but i bruised

it wasn't the violence
but the quiet
that left its mark
it wasn't the words
but the silence
that broke me apart

you never raised your hand
but your absence
left more scars than any blow could
your indifference
was the kind of hurt
that lasts long after
the pain fades

i bruised
because you didn't love me
the way i needed you to
and that was more painful
than anything you could've said

i kept calling it passion

the way we burned
through each other
the heat that kept us
coming back for more
i called it passion
because it felt like it
but in the end
it was only fire
that left nothing but ash

i mistook destruction
for desire
and chaos
for connection

i kept calling it passion
until it stopped feeling like love
and started feeling like survival

when it was just pain in disguise

we called it love
but it didn't feel like it
we called it passion
but it only burned
and left me raw

i mistook the fire
for something warm
but it was only the heat
of my own destruction
wrapped in a pretty bow
we never spoke the truth
because we didn't want to see it

it wasn't love
it was just pain
dressed up in the shape of desire
and i wore it like a mask
until i couldn't breathe anymore

i wanted to win you

i wanted to be the one
who could make you stay
the one who could fix
the cracks you tried to hide
i wanted to be the one
you couldn't walk away from
the one who could make you
believe in something real

but in my wanting
i lost myself
i wanted to win you
but i forgot
you were never mine to keep

but it wasn't a game

i thought i could win
if i played my cards right
if i gave enough of myself
maybe you'd stay
maybe i could be the answer
to the chaos you carried
but it wasn't a game
it was never about winning
it was about surviving
in a space
where love and loss
were never meant to coexist

i played with the rules
but the truth was
you were never a prize to be claimed
and i was never just a game
to be won

we didn't explode / we eroded

it wasn't the sudden impact
that broke us
it wasn't the crash
that shattered everything
it was the slow fade
the quiet wearing down
of everything we built
bit by bit
until there was nothing left
but dust in the cracks

we didn't explode
we eroded
until even the pieces
we wanted to keep
slipped through our fingers
without a sound

i lost myself with the lights on

i thought i could see clearly
but the brighter it got
the less i recognized
the reflection in front of me

i thought i was finding myself
but in the glow of your gaze
i became someone else
someone who didn't know
how to speak without fear
or love without losing pieces of herself

i lost myself
with the lights on
hoping i could see
but only drowning
in the shadows of who i was before

the match

you touched me

like a lit match

craving the burn

more than the warmth

The Fall

i saw it coming / and stayed anyway

i saw the cracks
before they broke us
i felt the distance
before we grew apart
but something in me
still wanted to stay
wanted to believe
the storm would pass
that we could outrun
the damage we were doing
to ourselves

i knew the end was coming
but i couldn't let go
of what we used to be
i saw it coming
and stayed anyway
because sometimes
love isn't enough
to make you leave
when you're already
so deep inside the mess

soft

it wasn't soft
like it used to be
it wasn't a whisper
or a breath
it was just a word
thrown into the space
between us
like a stone
shattering the silence

the last time you said my name
it felt more like goodbye
than anything we had ever said
before
and in that moment
i knew
we were already lost
even though
i still hadn't left

slowly

at first it was a few hours
then a day
then longer
until silence
became the only response
i could count on

i watched
as your words faded
like footsteps
disappearing in the sand
until i was left
talking to myself

i slept beside your absence

it wasn't your body
that i missed
but the warmth
the way you used to fill the space
with your breath
and your silence

i slept beside your absence
hoping it would become
something more
hoping i could fill the emptiness
with memories
but all that remained
was the coldness
of what was no longer here

and in the quiet of the night
i learned
how to sleep with loss
without ever waking up

emptiness

the bed was too wide
and the air too still
i reached for what wasn't there
my fingers grazing shadows
i thought i could hold
the space you left
but all i grasped
was emptiness

you kissed me with guilt on your breath

it wasn't a kiss
it was a confession
wrapped in desire
your lips said one thing
but your eyes told a different story

you kissed me with guilt
as if your touch
could erase the things
you had already taken
and left behind
as if i couldn't taste
the lies you had swallowed
before i ever came close

you kissed me
but it was never truly me
you wanted
it was just a way
to soothe your own remorse
for a love
you were never ready to give

i mistook silence for peace

when you stopped speaking
i thought we were healing
when the quiet stretched between us
i thought it was calm
but silence
wasn't the answer
it was a warning
that we were losing each other
one word at a time

i mistook silence
for peace
but it was just the space
where love used to be
and in that stillness
i learned
that sometimes
nothing is louder
than the things we never say

how to see me

once my name was familiar
once my smile was home
but somewhere
between the distance
and the silence
you forgot how to see me

there was someone else / there always was

i knew before you said it
i felt the shift in your touch
the way your eyes wandered
while mine stayed fixed on you
but i pretended not to notice
pretended that love could fill the gaps
where trust used to sit

there was someone else
you never had to name her
i saw her in the spaces
between your lies
and in the silence
that followed your words

there always was
someone else
and maybe
that's the way it was meant to be
a love
too quiet to fight for

your hands

i asked for your love
i begged for your time
i begged you to stay
but your hands
found their way to someone else

lie in the laundry

it wasn't the clothes
that told the story
it was the scent of someone else
clinging to the fabric
like a shadow
too stubborn to leave

i found your lie
in the laundry
folded neatly
next to the things
you swore were mine
but they weren't
and neither was the truth
you promised me every night

you washed it clean
but your lie
still stained the sheets

denial is a comfortable coffin

i wrapped myself in lies
like a blanket
the warmth of false hope
felt safer
than the cold truth

i closed my eyes
and pretended not to see
the cracks in the walls
the unraveling of everything
i thought i was holding together

denial is a comfortable coffin
a soft place to lie
while everything falls apart
but even the softest pillow
can't stop the weight of the truth
from suffocating you

favorite shirt

the one you bought me
the one that held your touch
in the fabric
and your laughter
in the threads

i cried in my favorite shirt
because it still smelled like you
but it didn't feel like home anymore
it felt like something
i had to leave behind
to move forward

i cried
because the shirt was all that remained
of the love
that was slipping through my fingers
and i couldn't hold onto it
no matter how tightly
i tried to keep it close

the mirror stopped recognizing me

i looked for myself in the glass
but found only pieces
of who i used to be
shattered
by the love
i thought would save me

the mirror stopped recognizing me
when i stopped recognizing my own worth
traded confidence
for compromise
traded truth
for the chance to stay

my voice cracked before my heart did

the words tried to leave
but trembled on the way out
a quiet
splintering sound
too soft to be a scream
too loud to be ignored

my voice cracked
before my heart did
as if my body knew
what was coming
before i did
as if grief was already
settling into my throat
before it reached my chest

you didn't flinch
didn't notice
how hard it was
for me to speak
while breaking

it wasn't just the loss / it was the way you left

you didn't slam the door
you didn't scream
you just
slowly
disappeared
like a shadow
slipping from under the light

no goodbye
no apology
just silence
and an empty room
where your love used to echo

it wasn't just the loss
it was the way you left
like i had never mattered
like we had been
nothing
like my heart
was something
you could outgrow

i kept replaying the goodbye

as if changing the angle
might soften the blow
as if hearing it again
might help it hurt less

but every time
your voice sounded colder
your eyes looked further
your hands more certain
about letting go

i kept replaying the goodbye
hoping to find
a reason
a hesitation
a flicker
that said
you wanted to stay

you didn't even look back

as if the years
meant nothing
as if i was just
a chapter
you were done reading

you didn't even look back
no pause
no second glance
just the sound of your shoes
walking away
from everything we built

and i stood there
waiting for a sign
a slip in your step
a shoulder turned
anything

i was angry / then numb

at first
i screamed into pillows
punched the air
wrote your name
with venom in my mouth

i cursed
every lie you fed me
every truth
you held back

but anger burns fast
and when it was gone
all that remained
was the quiet ache
of missing someone
i shouldn't miss

i was angry
then numb
because even rage
couldn't keep me
from feeling hollow
where you used to be

blank

because every word
reminded me of you

because the page
started to look
like your eyes
blank

suitcase in my chest

it did not knock
just let itself in
settled between my ribs
and made a home

hung old memories
on the walls of my lungs
so every breath
tasted like you

lined my spine
with all the words
i wish i had said
before the silence
swallowed them whole

grief unpacked its suitcase
in my chest
and i have been
living with the weight
of your leaving
ever since

the world kept going / how dare it

the sun rose
as if you didn't leave

traffic hummed
coffee brewed
strangers laughed in cafés
like my world
wasn't burning

i walked through days
like a ghost
watching people
live
as if love
doesn't end mid-sentence

the world kept going
and i wanted to scream
how dare you
keep spinning
when i am
still
standing
in the moment
you broke me

i forgot how to ask for help

because
somewhere
along the way
i learned
that needing
was too much
and hurting
was better done
quietly

the bed felt bigger than the room

without you in it
i could hear the space between us
stretching
until it swallowed
everything i thought i knew

the pillows
that once held your warmth
now felt like stone
the blankets
too empty
to shield me
from the cold you left behind

the bed felt bigger than the room
like it was begging me to fill
the silence
that used to feel like comfort
now felt like a weight
i couldn't lift

a ghost i fed

with every thought
every memory
i kept you alive
when all you ever were
was gone

i wrapped your name
in a blanket of longing
and whispered it into the dark
as if saying it aloud
would bring you back
as if i could resurrect
what you had buried

you became a ghost i fed
with the crumbs of myself
and i starved
waiting for you
to haunt me
in the way you once did

i hated you / then missed you / then both

first i burned with anger
because you left me in pieces
because i couldn't understand
why you took everything
and gave nothing in return

then the silence
turned to longing
and i missed the things
i swore i'd never miss
the way you smiled
the way you held me
like i mattered

and then i realized
i could still hate you
and miss you
at the same time
because love is complicated
and loss
is messy
and i never learned
how to let go of both

knives with good aim

they cut without warning
slice through the quiet
with the precision of a lover's touch
that once felt like safety
now feels like a wound

they find the places
you thought you'd forgotten
the hollow spots in your chest
where the ghosts of us still linger

memories are knives
and i never learned how to avoid them
how to shield myself
from the sharpness
that always comes
when i least expect it

i emptied myself trying to forget you

i poured out
the parts of me
that still held your name
still felt your touch
still wanted you
with every ache in my bones

i emptied myself
until there was nothing left
but the hollow echo
of a love i couldn't erase

but forgetting you
was not a river i could cross
no matter how much i spilled
no matter how many pieces
i gave away

because in the end
i learned
that even an empty heart
still remembers
what it used to hold

what did i even fall into

a web of promises
that tangled my thoughts
and wrapped itself
around my chest

a love that felt like gravity
but only pulled me downward
until i couldn't tell
if i was falling
or if i had already hit the ground

what did i even fall into
if not a lie
that looked too much
like truth
and felt too real
to ever leave?

rock bottom had your name carved in it

i hit the ground
and your voice
was the first thing i heard
calling my name
like a reminder
that you had always
been here
waiting for me to fall

rock bottom had your name carved in it

and every inch of it
felt like the echo
of every promise
you never kept

it wasn't the fall
that broke me
it was knowing
that even in the deepest dark
i was still looking for you

The Mirror

i didn't recognize myself

i looked in the mirror
and saw a girl
with tired eyes
and a mouth
that had forgotten
how to ask for more

i didn't recognize myself
not the way my shoulders curved inward
as if apologizing
for taking up space

you took pieces of me
and i let you
until what was left
was someone
i could not name

i asked the mirror who survived

she looked back at me
with cracked glass eyes
and a mouth
still trembling from silence

i asked the mirror
who survived
the love
the loss
the leaving

and it answered
not with words
but with the shape
of my spine—
still standing

fingerprints on my face

i didn't notice
until the mirror
showed me the lines
beneath my eyes
and the weight
that sorrow pressed
into my smile

grief left fingerprints
on my face
soft at first
like a touch
then deeper
like a bruise
that never turned yellow
just stayed

everywhere i go
i carry its trace
a face that remembers
even when i try
to forget

i wiped your name off my skin

it wasn't ink
but it stained
just the same

your name lived
on my collarbone
whispered down my arms
curled behind my knees

i scrubbed
and peeled
and bled
until it let go

even then
i could feel
the phantom letters
spell themselves
when the night got too quiet

i wiped your name
off my skin
but healing
never promised
forgetting

refunds

at first
i tried to return it
stuff it into boxes
leave it on strangers' doorsteps
write it out of my body

but grief
does not accept refunds

so i wear it
like a scar
with my name on it
not yours

i finally listened to myself

after years
of shushing the scream
beneath my smile

after telling my gut
she was overreacting
and making excuses
for my own ache

i finally
sat still
long enough
to hear the quiet voice
that never stopped speaking

she didn't beg
or yell

she simply said

leave

and for once
i did

waiting in the silence

it didn't arrive
with a bang
or a breakdown

just sat there
in the corner
of my quiet
like it had always been there

no dramatic exit
no final scream
just the absence
of pretending

when the noise stopped
and the room
was just me
and my breath
i saw it clearly

you weren't love
you were a lesson
i wasn't broken
i was becoming

disappearing for years

not all at once
but slowly
the way water
evaporates
when no one is looking

i shrank myself
to fit your comfort
silenced my voice
to soften your guilt

every time
i said "it's fine"
and swallowed
the storm
i lost another piece

until one day
i looked around
and didn't recognize
the outline
of the woman left

she was quieter
than i remembered
but she was still breathing
and that
was enough
to begin again

vanishing

if i have to
erase myself
just to be close to you

that is not closeness
that is collapse

if loving you
means
losing me

then what are we
really calling love

i was told

love is warm
a holding
a becoming

but with you
it felt more like
a slow disappearing
a quiet extinction

and i've learned

love should build
not blur
love should bloom
not burn

i named every wound

gave them titles
so they wouldn't feel so lost
each one
deserved a story
a reason
to exist

i gave them names
like regret
and shame
and betrayal
and with each one
i healed
a little slower
but a little stronger

i didn't forget them
but i learned
how to carry them
with grace

and none of them were yours alone

you left your mark
but you weren't the only one
to carve your name
into my skin

the weight of your absence
was heavy
but not the first
to settle there

i had others
who came before you
and some
who lingered after

you were one of many
who taught me pain
but not the last
to show me
how to heal

none of them
were yours alone
but you—
you were the one
who made me remember
how to survive

i kept saying i was fine / until i believed it

i wore the word
like a mask
a thin disguise
that slipped too easily
into my skin

i said it
when the cracks
were still fresh
when the pieces
didn't quite fit
but i kept repeating
the lie
until it wasn't a lie
anymore

until the ache
became a memory
i could no longer feel
until i was so used to pretending
i almost forgot
what real felt like

i kept saying i was fine
until one day
i realized
i had stopped waiting
to be anything else

healing is not forgetting

it is learning
to live with
the scar
and not the wound

it is knowing
the broken pieces
will never be perfect
but they are yours
and you are still whole

healing does not erase
the hurt
it simply makes room
for you to grow
around it

it does not ask you
to forget
it asks you
to remember
and choose to move forward
with the pieces you have left

healing is not forgetting
it is choosing
to not be defined
by what once broke you

romanticizing the war

it took me too long
to realize
the battle wasn't beautiful
it wasn't a story
of us against the world
but me against myself

i mistook the chaos
for passion
and the scars
for strength

i wanted the fire
without understanding
the burn
i craved the fight
without seeing
how much i bled

but now
i see the truth
the war wasn't love
it was survival
and i stopped romanticizing
the damage
when i realized
there was nothing heroic
about losing myself

i was the one who kept going back

i blamed you
for the ache
for the lies
for the breaking

but when the door closed
i was the one
who turned the handle
and opened it again

i told myself
i was done

but my hands kept reaching
and my heart kept forgiving

i was the one
who kept going back
because somewhere
in the pain
i thought
i could fix it

i thought
i could fix us

the chaos / the person

i don't miss your touch
i miss the electricity
the rush
the way i felt alive
even when it hurt

i don't miss your voice
i miss the way it filled
the empty spaces
like a storm
pouring into everything
and leaving nothing untouched

i don't miss the love
i miss the thrill
the unpredictability
the way i never knew
if i was flying
or falling

but the chaos
was never love
it was just noise
and i'm learning
to find silence
in the spaces you left

i forgave myself for staying

i blamed myself
for every moment
i should have walked away
but didn't

i thought
i was weak
for staying
in places
that hurt
in words
that cut
in arms
that never held me

but then
i realized
staying wasn't weakness
it was survival
it was trying
to make something whole
out of what was broken

i forgave myself
because healing
is a process
and sometimes
you have to stay
before you can go

this time / i chose me

i used to think
love was sacrifice
that giving myself away
was the only way
to show how much i cared

but this time
i chose me
i chose the parts
i had forgotten
i chose the voice
i had silenced
i chose the peace
i had abandoned

sit with the ache

at first
i ran from it
tried to bury it
with distractions
with empty words
with pretending
it didn't hurt

but it always came back
stronger
silent
heavy
like a visitor
who wouldn't leave

so i stopped fighting
and let it stay
i learned
the ache wasn't my enemy
it was part of me
a part that needed to be heard
not pushed away

i sat with it
i let it teach me
what i was capable of surviving
and slowly
i found peace
in its presence
and strength
in its silence

the mirror became a map

at first
i couldn't look
at the reflection
it felt too foreign
too broken
too far from who i once was

but then
i started to trace
the lines
the marks
the stories
etched into my skin

i realized
the cracks
weren't flaws
they were paths
leading me back to myself

the mirror
was no longer a judge
it became a guide
showing me
where i had been
and where i was still
learning to go

i stopped searching for who i was
and began to understand
who i was becoming

gentle

the scars used to feel like reminders
of pain i couldn't forget
marks of battles i lost
of pieces of myself
i thought i'd never find again

but as i traced them
with the softest touch
i realized
they weren't just wounds
they were proof
of my survival
of my strength
of how i kept going
even when i didn't know how

i traced them
and whispered thank you
to each one
for carrying me
through the storm

they were not mistakes
they were milestones
and now
i carry them with pride
because i am whole
because i am still here

i stopped asking why

i used to search for reasons
for the pain
for the losses
for the empty spaces
that never seemed to fill

i asked why
like it would make sense
like understanding
would make the hurt go away

but somewhere along the way
i stopped
i stopped needing to know
why it happened
why it hurt
why it wasn't fair

i stopped asking
and started accepting
that some things don't need answers
they just need to be lived through

so i let go
of the questions
and found peace
in the silence between them

and started asking what now

i used to wonder
why everything had to break
why i couldn't stop the falling
why i couldn't stop the hurt

but somewhere in the wreckage
i started asking
what now
what do i do with the pieces
what do i do with the lessons
what do i do with the strength
that came from surviving it all

and that question
changed everything
it was no longer about the past
about the why
but about the future
the healing
the rebuilding
the moving forward

so i stopped searching for answers
and started finding my way
one step
one breath
one day at a time

my reflection held me accountable

there was a time
i couldn't look
couldn't face
the eyes staring back at me
afraid of the truth they held
afraid of the mistakes
i refused to accept

but one day
i stood there long enough
to see past the shame
to see beyond the hurt
and the reflection
became a mirror of clarity
not judgment

it didn't forgive me
it didn't let me off easy
it simply asked
what will you do now
with all that you've learned

my reflection
didn't offer comfort
it offered honesty
and in that honesty
i found the strength
to rebuild
to try again
to be better

my reflection held me with grace

there was a time
when i saw only brokenness
in the mirror
when i judged myself
for the cracks
the scars
the softness

but one day
the reflection shifted
and the cracks
became the lines of wisdom
the scars were proof of survival

my reflection didn't punish me
it held me
with the kind of grace
i had forgotten to give myself

it whispered
you have always been worthy
of love
of peace
of healing

and in that moment
i learned
to hold myself
the same way

peace in the confrontation

i used to avoid the hard truths
hide from the things
that made my heart race
the conversations
the confrontations
the feelings i thought would break me

but one day
i stood in front of the hardest one
and spoke my truth
without hesitation
without apology

and for the first time
i didn't feel broken
i felt whole
i felt strong
i felt peace

the version of me you left behind is gone

the version of me
you left behind
is no longer holding onto you
she's found herself
in the quiet spaces
in the broken parts
in the strength
she never knew she had

this is not a comeback / this is a return

i didn't disappear
i just needed to be still
to find the pieces
that were lost
to remember who i was
before the world
tried to define me

this isn't a comeback
it's a return
to the self i almost forgot
to the fire
that never truly went out

i didn't need saving
i just needed silence
to hear my own voice again
to reclaim my space
to remember
that i am not a shadow
of who i used to be
but a version of myself
reborn

so this is not a comeback
it's the return
of the woman
who learned
how to stand tall
on her own
once more

i met myself for the first time

i didn't recognize
the woman in the mirror
her eyes were full of wisdom
but also wounds
her hands were tired
but still reaching
her heart was soft
but scarred

she wasn't who i thought i'd become
she was more
she was everything i had been
and everything i was still becoming

i met myself for the first time
and realized
i had always been here
hidden beneath the hurt
beneath the doubts
beneath the fears
waiting to be seen

i finally saw her
the woman who survived
who thrived
who loved
who let go
who held on
and who kept going

and i said / finally

i said it out loud
for the first time
with no fear
with no apology

finally
i am who i was meant to be
finally
i am no longer hiding
behind the mask
of someone else's expectations

finally
i have shed the weight
of the past
the wounds that once defined me
are now stories
of survival
not scars of defeat

finally
i am whole
finally
i am mine

The Armor

i didn't need saving / i needed space

i didn't need someone to rescue me
i needed to breathe
without the weight of expectations
without the pressure of being enough
for someone else

i didn't need saving
i needed the silence
to hear my own heart
the room to grow
the time to understand
who i was
when i was alone
and not defined by someone else's love

i didn't need saving
i needed space
to rebuild
to trust myself again
to learn the strength
that was always inside me

and in that space
i found my armor
not forged by someone else
but crafted by my own hands

this time / i stitched myself

i didn't wait for someone
to mend the pieces
i gathered the fragments of me
and carefully threaded them back together
with hands that knew pain
but also knew healing

i stitched the cracks
with threads of resilience
the gaps
with moments of self-love
each stitch
a promise
that i would never let myself fall apart again

i didn't wait for a savior
this time
i became my own

i rebuilt my heart
my strength
my voice
i pieced together the fragments
that were once broken
and turned them into armor

healing isn't pretty / but it's mine

it's not neat
or wrapped in ribbons
it doesn't follow a timeline
or fit the image
of what others expect

it's messy
and it's raw
and some days
i still feel the weight of the wounds
that haven't completely healed
but that's okay
because it's mine

it's not graceful
it's stumbling
it's falling
and getting up again
it's shedding the skin
of who i was
and learning
how to love who i've become

healing isn't pretty
but it's mine
and i wear it
with pride
with patience
with the quiet understanding
that it's a journey
not a destination

i built boundaries instead of walls

i used to believe
that love meant surrender
that to protect my heart
i had to shut others out
but that only left me
with a hollow silence
and a heart that forgot how to trust

so i built boundaries instead of walls
i carved lines
where the love could flow
but the hurt couldn't stay
i learned that boundaries
weren't meant to isolate
but to protect
to let the right things in
and keep the wrong ones out

i built boundaries
that said
"you can come this far
but no further"
i built them with care
and with the knowing
that i am worthy of love
that doesn't leave scars

boundaries are not fences
they are gates with purpose
inviting in what nourishes me
and turning away what doesn't

no is a full sentence

i don't owe an explanation
when i say no
it doesn't need to be justified
it doesn't need to be followed by
"but i really want to"
or "i feel bad for saying this"

no is complete
no is enough
no is a boundary i've learned to set
without apology
without guilt

i don't need to explain
why i'm not ready
why i'm not interested
why i'm not okay
my no is my power
my no is my truth
and that's all that matters

no is a full sentence
and i don't need anything more
to make it true

i stopped bleeding for people who never asked

i used to give
everything i had
even when it left me empty
even when i was left broken
they never asked for my hurt
they never asked for my love
but i gave it anyway

i bled for them
but they never saw
the scars were mine to carry
the wounds were mine to heal

i stopped bleeding
for people who never asked
because i realized
my blood is sacred
my heart is sacred
and giving it away
without a second thought
was a kind of violence
i didn't deserve to do to myself

now i keep my heart safe
for those who will hold it with care
for those who will ask
if it's okay to love me

softness is not weakness

i used to think
that softness was something
to hide
that tenderness made me
vulnerable
that love and kindness
were things to be cautious of

but i have learned
softness is strength
it takes courage
to stay open
to love with no guarantee
to be kind when the world
expects hardness

i have learned
that gentleness is a shield
not a flaw
it doesn't make me weak
it makes me human
it makes me resilient
it makes me brave enough
to face the world
with compassion
even when the world is cruel

strength doesn't always roar

strength is not always loud
it doesn't always shout
it doesn't always rise
in a blaze of fury

sometimes strength is the silence
after the storm
the quiet resilience
that keeps you standing
when you want to fall

sometimes strength is simply
getting up each day
when the weight of the world
pulls you down
and still,
you find a way to move forward

strength doesn't always roar
sometimes it whispers
it hides in the small moments
the gentle refusal
to give up on yourself
even when no one is watching

strength is the peace
you make with your own heart
the patience you give to yourself
the quiet power of surviving
even when it feels like you're breaking

i learned to walk away sooner

i used to linger
in places that didn't feel like home
i stayed longer than i should
in the rooms that made me shrink
and in hearts that made me doubt my worth

i let love twist
and turn until it broke
i thought if i waited long enough
it would fix itself
but all it did was pull me apart

so now
i walk away sooner
before the cracks can become too deep
before the silence becomes too loud
before the love turns into something
that doesn't recognize me

i have learned
that leaving doesn't make me weak
it makes me strong
it makes me whole again
because the person who deserves my presence
will never make me feel small

i stopped explaining my worth

i no longer spend my energy
proving i am enough
to the ones who can't see it
i stopped explaining
why i deserve respect
why my time is valuable
why my heart is not for taking

i stopped explaining my worth
to the ones who think silence is weakness
and boundaries are demands
to the ones who expect love to be endless
without ever giving anything in return

i stopped explaining my worth
because it's not for you to understand
it is not a puzzle for you to solve
it is not something i have to justify
to anyone who doesn't see it
or feel it in their bones

you don't have to understand to respect it

you don't have to understand
to respect it
my strength
my silence
my choices
my boundaries

it doesn't require your approval
just your recognition

you don't need to comprehend
to honor
the way i protect myself
the way i show up
the way i love
the way i leave

because respect
isn't earned by agreement
it is earned by simply seeing
and allowing space
for what is
without demanding it to be something else

you don't have to understand
you just need to respect
and that is enough

i love without losing myself now

i no longer disappear
when love comes my way
no longer bend
until my bones crack
no longer give pieces of me
until there's nothing left

i love
but i stay intact
i love
but i do not break
i love
but i hold my own hand
even when i reach for yours

i love
but i love myself first
i love
and i am still here
whole
complete

i let go without begging to be held

i didn't hold on tighter
didn't beg you to stay
i let my hands open
letting go was not weakness
it was freedom

i didn't chase you down
didn't drown in silence
i let the space between us
become the breath
that fills me again

i let go
without feeling desperate
without feeling incomplete
because i learned
my worth is not tied
to anyone's touch
or their absence

i let go
because i can stand on my own
without asking for permission
to exist fully
to love fully
to live fully

i let go
and the universe caught me
with open arms of peace

forgiveness doesn't mean return

i forgave you
but that doesn't mean
i'll open the door
to the harm you caused

forgiveness is freedom
it's releasing the grip
of anger
but it's not an invitation
to step back into my life

i forgave you
not for you
but for me
to let go of the weight
so i could breathe again

forgiveness doesn't erase the past
it doesn't rewrite the wrongs
it just untangles the hold
that kept me tethered
to what i couldn't change

you don't have to return
to be forgiven
but i do have to return to myself
to keep moving forward

i outgrew the version of me that needed you

there was a time
when i thought i couldn't breathe
without your approval
when i believed
i was smaller
without your validation

but i grew
in ways you couldn't see
and outgrew the me
that held onto you
like a lifeline

resilience is muscle memory

i built myself
with the quiet strength of repetition
one small step at a time
until my heart knew how to rise
even when the ground shook beneath me

i learned to stand
before the storm could ask me to kneel
and i learned to breathe
even when the weight of it all
pressed too heavy on my chest

resilience
isn't always loud
it's the gentle pull of the tide
after every crash
it's the muscle memory
of standing up again
without asking for permission

i don't miss who i was / she got me here

i don't miss who i was
she got me here
the version of me that burned with questions
that held on tight to what she thought she needed
she was fierce in her search for answers
even if they came with scars

but now
i stand taller than i ever thought possible
and i see her in the mirror
not as someone i wish to become again
but as the strength that shaped me

i don't miss the fear
or the doubt
or the weight of trying to be someone else
i don't need to apologize to her
because without her
i wouldn't have the courage
to walk this path
with the confidence i carry today

she was the spark
and now i'm the fire
that continues to burn
but on my own terms

grace over grudges

i chose grace
not because i forgot
but because i grew
and holding onto the hurt
only kept me chained to a past
that no longer serves me

grudges weigh down the heart
they are heavy stones
carried around
until you realize
you don't have to keep holding them

so i let them slip
one by one
into the river of release
and watched as they disappeared
into the current of forgiveness

grace isn't forgetting
it's choosing peace
despite the wounds
and finding freedom
in the spaces
where anger once lived

i will never regret choosing grace
it has taught me
to move forward
with lighter steps
and a heart that can finally breathe

not every lesson needs revisiting

some lessons are scars
that heal best when left untouched
you don't need to open the wound
to remember the pain
you don't need to relive the storm
to know how the wind felt

i learned
that some things
are better left in the past
not because i forgot them
but because i outgrew them

i stopped performing peace

i used to wear it
like a costume
smiling through the chaos
like it was something i had to prove

pretending to be whole
when my pieces were scattered
telling myself it was enough
to just look calm

but peace isn't a show
it's not a mask
it's not an act you put on
to make others comfortable

i stopped performing peace
and started living it
quietly
in the way i breathe
in the spaces i choose to keep
in the moments i let myself break

real peace doesn't ask for applause
it asks for honesty
and sometimes
that means leaving
the performance
behind

this softness has teeth

i learned to love
with the fierceness of a storm
but with the gentleness of a whisper
softness doesn't mean surrender

i am the quiet
that follows the loudest wars
i am the calm
before a powerful wave crashes

this softness isn't weakness
it's a weapon in disguise
it's the grace of a lioness
before she pounces

you mistake my silence
for submission
you mistake my stillness
for fear

but this softness
has teeth
and it will tear through the lies
it will bite back
when you forget who i am

i wear my healing like armor

i didn't find strength in the fight
i found it in the quiet spaces
in the moments where i chose myself
again and again

i wear my healing like armor
not to shield me from the world
but to remind me of what i've survived
what i've become
through the cracks and the tears

it doesn't glisten
or sparkle
it's worn
like a well-loved coat
with every stitch
a memory of resilience

and though the world still tries to break me
i stand stronger
because i know
that even in the scars
there is power

i am not who you remember

you left when i was still breaking
but i have rebuilt
brick by brick
a version of me
you can no longer recognize

i have grown in the silence
learned the language of my own heart
and now
i speak in the words of freedom
not the whispers of fear

i am not the girl you left behind
her ghost still lingers
but she has become
a part of the past
a lesson i learned
but no longer carry

so when you return
looking for pieces of her
you will find only
the woman i am now
stronger
wiser
whole

there's power in silence

i used to fill the space
with words
hoping they would heal
the parts of me
too afraid to speak

but now
i sit with the quiet
and listen
to the language of my soul
whispering truths
no sound could capture

i learned to rest without guilt

i used to fill every moment
with action
fearing stillness
would be mistaken for weakness
but now
i allow myself to pause
without the weight of shame

rest is not surrender
it is reclaiming
the parts of me
that once ran on empty
it is breathing
without checking
the clock for permission

i learned that healing
requires space
and gentleness
and i am deserving
of both

i protect my joy like it's sacred

i guard my happiness
with the same intensity
as one would hold
a flame in the wind
not every moment is meant
to be shared
not every conversation
deserves my light

i've learned
that joy is a fragile thing
it thrives in spaces
free from expectation
and in the absence
of those who would dim it

so i cherish it
and keep it close
only letting it unfold
with those who know
how to honor
what's precious

it is not selfish
to protect the things
that make you whole
sometimes
the only person
who needs to understand
the value of your peace
is you

peace is the loudest thing i own

it doesn't scream
it doesn't shout
it doesn't demand
to be heard

it fills the spaces
where noise once lived
and in its stillness
i find strength

peace is the weight
i carry with pride
because it has
never needed
to prove itself

it speaks
with a certainty
that makes the world
seem smaller
and my heart
feel larger

and i know now
there is no treasure
greater than the quiet
i've claimed as my own

i don't flinch when i look back

i don't flinch
when i look back
i simply nod
to the version of me
who got me here

and i thank her
for every step
she took
even when it was
the hardest thing
to do

i built a home in myself

i painted my walls
with kindness
hung mirrors
that reflected my truth
and lit candles
that warmed my spirit

i became the roof
that shields my heart
the door
i choose to open
when it's time to let love in
and the lock
i turn when i need
space to breathe

my home is not perfect
but it's mine
and every corner
holds the quiet
of my own peace

i built a home in myself
and for the first time
i know what it means
to belong
to me

after every war

it’s not the scars
that tell the story
but the way i stand
with my face turned
toward the light
even when the shadows
still follow me

it’s not the battle
i fought with the world
but the quiet peace
i found within myself
after every war
i survived

this is what survival looks like in sunlight

i don't wear my pain
like a badge anymore
i wear it
like a second skin
that i've learned to live in
with grace
and without apology

this is what survival looks like
in sunlight
it's waking up
and choosing to bloom
even when the earth beneath me
still feels unsteady
it's stepping forward
with trembling legs
but with the courage
to keep going

this is what it looks like
to heal and to rise
to rise from the rubble
and find beauty in the ruins
to remember
that after every storm
the sun does come back
and so do i

The Rise

i woke up different

i woke up different
as if the sky had whispered
to my bones
that today
was the day
i would no longer
be afraid of the sunlight

the weight of yesterday
fell off me
like a skin too tight
and in its place
i found strength
i never knew
could fit this well

i didn't recognize
the woman in the mirror
but i smiled anyway
because
she looked
like someone
who had learned
how to rise
from everything
that tried
to break her

not healed / but holy

not healed
but holy
still scarred
but whole

broken parts

i have learned
to love the broken parts
as much as the mended ones
because they tell a story
of survival
of becoming
of bending
without breaking

i am not flawless
but i am enough
woven together
from the threads of struggle
and strength

i have found grace
in the gaps
where i thought i had lost myself
and now
i stand
not as a perfect woman
but as a woman
who knows her worth
even in the cracks

i started over with fire in my lungs

i started over
with fire in my lungs
and ashes in my hands
burned from what i once was
but glowing with what i could be

i breathed in the flames
until they became my air
until they fueled me
until they no longer scared me

i built myself
from the heat
and from the ruins
learning that destruction
does not always mean the end
sometimes
it is just the beginning

i started over
not because i had to
but because i could
and this time
i chose to rise
from the ashes
with fire in my lungs
and nothing to prove
but everything to live for

the girl who broke became the woman who built

the girl who broke
became the woman who built

with every crack
she learned how to mold
her pieces into strength
until the brokenness
was just the foundation

the rubble beneath her feet
became the ground she stood on
and from it
she grew roots
stronger than any storm

the girl who once crumbled
now stands tall
a testament to what happens
when you stop waiting
for someone else to rebuild you

she built herself
brick by brick
and now
she is unshakable

they buried me / they didn't know i was a seed

they thought
i would wither
under the weight of their silence

but i grew
in the dark
rooted in resilience
nourished by the pain
they tried to bury me in

each struggle
became the sun
each tear
the rain

and from the earth
i emerged
stronger
wilder
rooted in my truth

they buried me
but i am not what they thought
i am the forest
that grew
from their mistake

i wrote my own resurrection

i wrote my own resurrection
with every scar
every broken piece
became a line of verse

i rebuilt myself
from the ashes of who i used to be
and when i rose
it wasn't just to survive
it was to live
to roar
to take up space

i became the story
they never expected
but always needed
to know that even in the dark
i could find my own light
and write myself back
to the world

every version of me led here

every version of me led here
to this moment
to this quiet power
that no one could take from me
not the past
not the pain
not the doubt

each mistake
each tear
each broken dream
was a step
a map
a part of the journey

and when i look back
i see all the versions of myself
holding hands
bringing me to this
stronger
braver
whole
version
who finally knows
i am enough

the glow-up wasn't just skin deep

the glow-up wasn't just skin deep
it was in the way
i stopped shrinking
in the way i started choosing myself
over the things that tried to break me
it was in the way i found my voice
and learned to use it
without apology

it was in the way
i built from the rubble
and rose with more than just
a pretty face
but a heart that knows
its own worth
and a soul that no longer
fears the light

map of my freedom

i spread my arms
and let my body
be the map of my freedom
i filled every corner
of my own world
and breathed in the air
that was always mine
to claim

i became the closure

i became the closure
i once searched for
in places
that didn't honor me

i stopped waiting
for apologies
that would never come
and gave myself
the peace
that was always mine
to claim

i closed the door
with grace
and left behind
the chapters
that didn't serve me
writing my own ending
with every step forward

you don't get to name my strength

you don't get to name my strength
just because you couldn't understand
how i carried myself
through storms you never saw
or felt the weight
of my quiet resilience

my power is not for you to define
it is not measured
by the space you think i should take
or the voice you think i should have
it is mine to own
mine to rise with
without permission
without explanation

they watched / but i soared anyway

they watched
as i spread my wings
waiting for me to fall
but i soared anyway

with every doubt
i silenced their whispers
with every fear
i flew higher

they thought my wings were fragile
but i was made of strength
they never saw
and i became the sky
i was always meant to touch

i stopped whispering my power

i stopped whispering my power
like it was something
to be ashamed of

no longer shrinking
so others feel tall
no longer dimming
to keep them comfortable

i say my name
with my whole chest now
because i am not an echo
i am the sound

no one had to lose for me to win

no one had to lose
for me to win

this is not a race
it is a return
to who i've always been

your light doesn't dim mine
my joy doesn't steal yours

we can rise
side by side
and still
touch the sky

i unlearned shame

i unlearned shame
the way you peel
layers of an old skin

it didn't fall off
i had to rip it
gently
daily
with both hands

until i stood bare
and still worthy

until i looked at myself
and didn't flinch
at the softness
i used to hide

grace found me in motion

grace found me in motion
not when i was still
but mid-step
mud on my shoes
and breath catching in my chest

it met me
not in perfection
but in the trying
in the trembling
in the way i kept
moving anyway

i became my own proof

i became my own proof
that survival
can look like softness
and power
can wear a quiet smile

i stopped needing
permission
to bloom
and bloomed anyway

i am not
what they said
i couldn't be
i am
what i always was
before they made me doubt it

success looks good on my scars

they said
i'd never make it out whole

but here i am
in heels
on stages
in peace

wearing every wound
like a medal
not because it didn't hurt
but because i kept moving

my scars
did not shrink me
they shaped me

and now
even the pain
claps for me

not revenge / just growth

i didn't come back
to prove you wrong

i came back
to prove myself right

this isn't
a victory lap
around your silence

this is
the quiet bloom
of someone
who chose healing
over hate

who outgrew
the need
to be seen
by eyes
that never looked
with love

i didn't return / i arrived

this is not a comeback
this is a becoming

i did not crawl
back to where i was
i stepped forward
into who i am

no longer seeking
a seat at the table
i built my own

and sat in it
like a woman
who finally
knows
she belongs

joy started feeling safe again

i stopped looking
over my shoulder
every time i laughed

as if happiness
was something
i had to pay for later

now
i let it in
without apology

joy curled up beside me
like it always belonged
and this time
i didn't flinch when it stayed

i loved loudly / including myself

i stopped apologizing
for the way my love
poured out
like rivers
too wild to be contained

i loved loudly
with no hesitation
with no fear
of being too much

i loved me
with the same fierceness
and the same grace

and for the first time
i heard it
i heard my own love
echo back
and it was enough

i built an empire from ashes

they thought i was broken
but i was just
gathering
what remained
and using it
to build what they said
couldn't be done

i took the pieces
of my past
and made them
the foundation
of my future

each scar a brick
each tear a tower

and now
i stand
taller
stronger
than anything
they ever tried to tear down

i didn't win the war / i ended it

i fought
not for victory
but for peace
the kind that comes
when you stop
trying to break
what is already whole

i didn't win
because there was nothing left to conquer
the battle was never with them
it was always with myself

so i laid down
my weapons
and found freedom
in the quiet
that followed

my peace is permanent

i no longer search for calm
in the chaos
it lives inside me now
a quiet thunder
steady
and sure

i don't need to make excuses
or apologize for it
this peace
is mine to keep
a home i've built
in the silence of my soul

it will not fade
it will not bend
it is permanent
like the sun's promise
to rise every day

i don't chase anymore / i choose

i used to run after things
as if my worth
depended on their arrival
but now
i stand still
and let what's meant for me
come

i don't chase people
or moments
i choose what stays
what aligns with my peace
and what nurtures
my growth

i no longer beg for attention
i simply make space
for what chooses me
to stay
and stay with intention

there's sunlight in my spine now

once my back was bent
under the weight of others' expectations
but now
there's sunlight in my spine
a warmth that stretches
through the cracks
and fills the space they left behind

i stand tall
not because i have to
but because i finally know
how to hold myself
without apology

my bones are strong
with the strength of every storm i've survived
and every light i've let in
now i rise
with sunlight in my spine
and nothing can dim it

i stopped surviving / i started creating

i used to wait for the storm to pass
hoping the skies would clear
now
i make my own weather
i paint the clouds
with colors of my choosing

no longer just existing
i began to bloom
from the inside out
learning that survival is not enough
creation is what saves me

i don't wait for permission
i don't wait for calm
i carve my own path
with the power of what i build
and the courage to make it beautiful

this is what rising looks like

i was the one who fell
but i am the one who rises
not because i have to
but because i know how

i turned my pain
into my foundation
my scars
are the lines that guide me up

there is nothing soft
about this ascent
it's gritty
it's messy
it's loud with every step

i am not just surviving
i am becoming
the version of me
that i always knew i could be

i am not a phoenix / i burned and bloomed

i didn't rise from the ashes
i walked through the fire
and found my own strength
in the heat of it all

i wasn't reborn
i grew
rooted in the soil of my struggle

the flames didn't give me life
they taught me how to live
they taught me
how to bloom
in the mess of it all

i am not a phoenix
i am the fire
and the flower
all at once

Made in the USA
Columbia, SC
07 June 2025

1e470a8f-d4fd-4bb8-ba8c-750a02b9e926R01